WINGS, HORNS, & CLAWS

A DINOSAUR BOOK OF EPIC PROPORTIONS

Also by Christopher Wormell

The New Alphabet of Animals
Teeth, Tails, & Tentacles: An Animal Counting Book
Mice, Morals, & Monkey Business: Lively Lessons From Aesop's Fables
Through The Animals' Eyes: The Story of The First Christmas

WINGS, HORNS, & CLAWS

A DINOSAUR BOOK OF EPIC PROPORTIONS
BY CHRISTOPHER WORMELL

RUNNING PRESS

PHILADELPHIA · LONDON

9 8 7 6 5 4 3 2 1
Digit on the right indicates the number of this printing

Library of Congress Control Number: 2006938053

ISBN-13: 978-0-7624-2419-1
ISBN-10: 0-7624-2419-2

Cover an interior design by Joshua McDonnell
Edited by Kelli Chipponeri
Typography: ITC Berkeley

This book may be ordered by mail from the publisher.
Please include $2.50 for postage and handling.
But try your bookstore first!

Published by Running Press Kids, an imprint of
Running Press Book Publishers
2300 Chestnut Street
Philadelphia, PA 19103-4371

Visit us on the web!
www.runningpress.com

For Jack,

who was promised this book fifteen years ago,
is all grown up now, and probably doesn't know
his Allosaurus from his Ankylosaurus!

COMPSOGNATHUS
(Comp-sog-nay-thuss)

was a very small dinosaur, about the size of a chicken.

DIMORPHODON
(Dy-morf-oh-don)

had a large, puffin–like beak—as well as teeth.

OVIRAPTOR
(Oh-vi-rap-tor)

was thought to be an egg thief.

PROTOCERATOPS
(Proe-toe-serr-a-tops)

had a large bony shield,
which protected its neck
when attacked.

DEINONYCHUS
(Dye-non-ee-kuss)

means "terrible claw."

PACHYCEPHALOSAURUS
(Pack-ih-sef-ah-low-sawr-us)

would head-butt rivals with his thick dome-like skull.

GALLIMIMUS
(Gal-i-miem-us)

was a bird like dinosaur with long legs, a slender body, and beak–like jaws.

PTERANODON

(Ter-an-o-don)

was a flying reptile
with huge bat-like wings.

STEGOSAURUS

(Steg-o-sawr-us)

had a crest of bony plates along its back.

TRICERATOPS
(Try-ser-a-tops)

was the largest of the
horned dinosaurs.

ANKYLOSAURUS
(Ang-kie-lo-sawr-us)

liked to swing the huge club at the end of its tail.

ALLOSAURUS
(Al-oh-sawr-us)

was one of the largest carnivores.

ELASMOSAURUS
(Il-az-mow-sawr-us)

lived in the ocean and had flippers like fish fins.

TYRANNOSAURUS REX

(Tie-ran-o-sawr-us Rex)

was a fearsome predator
with teeth 9 inches long.

DIPLODOCUS
(Di-plod-o-kus)

had a long whip–like tail
and small rod–like teeth.

ARGENTINOSAURUS
(Ahr-gen-teen-oh-sawr-us)

may have been the largest
dinosaur of all.

But perhaps there were
bigger ones...

Most dinosaurs,
no matter how big or small,
hatched from eggs.

Specific Dinosaurs Featured in This Book

COMPSOGNATHUS
(Comp-sog-nay-thuss)

Compsognathus was about 28 inches long and is one of the smallest dinosaurs ever found. It lived 145-155 million years ago and probably ate insects and other small creatures. The long legs and long tail suggest it was a fast runner and used its tail for balance. It is thought he could walk on 2 or 4 legs. Compsognaythus may have lived in herds and was a herbivore—a plant eater. The name Compsognaythus means "pretty jaw." Fossils of this creature have been found in France and Germany.

DIMORPHODON
(Dy-morf-oh-don)

Dimorphodon was not a dinosaur but a Pterosaur, which means "winged lizard." It lived around 190 million years ago, had a wingspan of about 4 feet, and probably ate fish and small mammals. Fossils of this reptile were found in Dorset, England, in 1828 by one of the first fossil hunters: Mary Anning. The name Dimorphodon means "two-form tooth," which refers to the two distinct types of teeth this dinosaur had; those at the front were long and protruded from its beak, while those at the back were much smaller.

OVIRAPTOR
(Oh-vi-rap-tor)

This dinosaur was about 8 feet long and lived roughly 80 million years ago. The first fossils of Oviraptor were found in Mongolia, and discovered along with fossilised broken eggshells. It was thought that the strong, curved beak-like jaws of this reptile were used to crack the eggs of other dinosaurs. More recently, however, tests have proved that the fossil eggs were those of Oviraptor itself. So its name, which means "egg thief," is perhaps a little unfair!

PROTOCERATOPS
(Proe-toe-serra-tops)

Protoceratops was one of the first of the horned dinosaurs—its name meaning "first horned face." Though it did not actually have any proper horns itself, it did have the large neck shield common to these dinosaurs. At about 8 feet it was one of the smallest of the horned group and lived nearly 80 million years ago. Fossils of Protoceratops have been found in Mongolia and China.

DEINONYCHUS
(Dye-non-ee-kuss)

This dinosaur was named for the very large, curved, blade-like claw in the second toe of each foot. Deinonychus means "terrible claw." It was about 10 feet long and may have hunted in a pack, attacking much larger dinosaurs. It lived about 110 million years ago and fossils of Deinonychus have been found in North America.

PACHYCEPHALOSAURUS
(Pack-ih-sef-ah-low-sawr-us)

Pachycephalosaurus was about 15 feet long and its name means "thick headed lizard." It's easy to see why—the skull of this dinosaur was up to 10 inches thick where it rose to form a large dome on the top of its head. Although we don't know for sure what the rest of Pachycephalosaurus looked like, as only skulls have been found, we can be fairly certain that they used their skulls for head-butting! Fossils have been found in Western North America, where it lived around 70 million years ago.

GALLIMIMUS
(Gal-i-miem-us)

Gallimimus bones were found in the Gobi Desert in Mongolia, where it lived approximately 75 million years ago. Gallimimus means "rooster mimic" but at 13-20 feet long, standing two-to-three times as high as a man, with long legs and a long neck, this dinosaur was probably more like a very large ostrich than a rooster. Gallimimus was an omnivore—eating both plants and animals—surviving mostly on insects, lizards, eggs, and some plants.

PTERANODON
(Ter-an-o-don)

Its name means "winged and toothless" for it had a large beak rather like a pelican, which it must have used to scoop up fish from the surface waters of the ocean. Pteranodon was one of the largest of the flying reptiles, with a wingspan that stretched up to 33 feet. Pteranodon lived 75-85 million years ago and its fossils have been found in North America and Europe.

STEGOSAURUS
(Steg-o-sawr-us)

This dinosaur lived around 145 million years ago and had two rows of large bony plates along the ridge of its humped back. These may have been used for self-defence, to regulate the animals body heat, or perhaps they were just for show, nobody really knows. We do know, however, that even though Stegosaurus was roughly 30 feet long, it had a tiny brain—only about the size of a walnut. Stegosaurus means "plated lizard" and fossils of this dinosaur have been found in Western North America, Europe, Southeast Asia, and Southern Africa.

TRICERATOPS
(Try-ser-a-tops)

Triceratops was 30 feet long and the largest of the horned dinosaurs. Its name means "three horned face" and its skull, including the large neck shield, could measure up to 10 feet—one of the largest skulls of all dinosaurs. Triceratops was a plant eater and roamed North America in large herds 70 million years ago.

ANKYLOSAURUS
(Ang-kie-lo-sawr-us)

Ankylosaurus was armoured like a tank. It had bony plates and spikes covering its back, and a heavy club at the end of its tail, which it must have used as a defensive weapon to smash the heads or legs of attacking carnivores. The name Ankylosaurus means "fused lizard" as its armour plating and spikes were fused into its skin. It was about 35 feet long and lived nearly 70 million years ago. Fossils of this creature have been found in Western North America.

ALLOSAURUS
(Al-oh-sawr-us)

Allosaurus was a meat eater, which preyed on dinosaurs like Stegosaurus and Iguanodon, more than 150 million years ago. Its name means "different lizard" as the vertebrae of this dinosaur were lighter than the vertebrae of other dinosaurs. At approximately 40 feet long Allosaurus was one of the largest carnivores of its time. Fossils have been found in North America, Europe, Africa, and Australia.

ELASMOSAURUS
(Il-az-mow-sawr-us)

This reptile was not a dinosaur but a Plesiosaur, which means "close to lizard," as these creatures were lizard like but had flippers instead of legs. Elasmosaurus, at 46 feet, was one of the largest Plesiosaurs, though about half its body length was its extremely long neck. Elasmosaurus means "thin plated lizard," and refers to the thin, plate-like bones in its pelvis.

TYRANNOSAURUS REX

(Tie-ran-o-sawr-us Rex)

Tyrannosaurus Rex was about 40 feet long with massive, powerful back legs and very small two fingered arms. With its enormous head and four-foot jaws, filled with replaceable teeth up to 9 inches long, Tyrannosaurus Rex certainly was the "tyrant lizard king" of its name. Fossils of this dinosaur have been found in Western North America and Mongolia, where it preyed upon plant eaters like the great Sauropods roughly 75 million years ago.

DIPLODOCUS

(Di-plod-o-kus)

Diplodocus was an incredible 90 feet long, and was one of the longest dinosaurs that ever lived. Its name means "double beam" and refers to the tail, which had an extra bone beneath each vertebra to strengthen it and protect the blood vessels within. Dipodocus may have used its extra long tail, which tapered to a fine tip, as a kind of whip when attacked. Many fossils have been found of this dinosaur in Western North America, where it lived approximately 150 million years ago.

ARGENTINOSAURUS

(Ahr-gen-teen-oh-sawr-us)

Argentinosaurus roamed the earth 100 million years ago. From the few bones so far discovered it seems that Argentinosaurus may have been the largest dinosaur that ever lived. It could have been 130 feet long! The few bones—back bones and leg bones—were discovered in Argentina, hence its name "Argentina Lizard." Very little is known about this creature, but it's fairly certain that a dinosaur of this size would have needed to eat several tons of food a day.

Do you notice anything interesting about Compsognathus—the little dinosaur at the beginning of this book?

That's right! He's not *just* at the beginning of the book, he pops up in all the pictures!

Why do you think he is there?

And why does he get smaller and smaller throughout the book?

You see dinosaurs vary in size. Some are quite small, while some are absolutely enormous! Compsognathus really shouldn't be in some of the pictures, because he wasn't around when some of the other dinosaurs were alive. He would never have dodged the deadly jaws or Tyrannosaurus Rex or avoided the titanic tread of Argentinosaurus. These dinosaurs lived in a time millions of years after Compsognathus had disappeared from the earth. But by putting other dinosaurs next to Compsognathus, who was the size of a chicken, we get a better idea of how big the other dinosaurs really were.

Christopher Wormell is a leading English wood engraver. Inspired by the works of Thomas Bewick, he took up wood engraving in 1982, and has since illustrated several books in addition to his work in the fields of advertising, design, and editorial illustrations.

Long before Christopher became a wood engraver he was taught lino-cutting by his father, mainly for the mass production of Christmas cards. Around Christmastime the Wormell household became something of a cottage industry with Christopher and his brothers and sisters producing handmade cards by the hundred.

His first book for children, *An Alphabet of Animals,* started as a series of simple, lino-cut illustrations for his son Jack, and eventually grew into a book that took the Graphics Prize at the Bologna International Children's Book Fair in 1991 and spawned a sequel, *The New Alphabet of Animals.* Most recently, Christopher has received acclaim for his animal counting book *Teeth, Tails, & Tentacles,* which was named a *New York Times Book Review* Best Illustrated Children's Book, an American Library Association Notable Book, and a Kirkus Reviews 2004 Editor's Choice, among others. Some of Christopher's other children's book credits include *Mowgli's Brothers, Blue Rabbit and Friends, Blue Rabbit and the Runaway Wheel, Animal Train, Off to the Fair, George and the Dragon, Two Frogs, In the Woods, The Big Ugly Monster and the Little Stone Rabbit,* and *Swan Song,* a collection of poems by J. Patrick Lewis about extinct animals.

He lives in London with his wife and three children.